GUITAR • VOCAL

STRUM & SING

MUSIC FROM THE MOTION PICTURE SOUNDTRACK

R★CKETMAN

ISBN 978-1-5400-6288-8

HAL•LEONARD®

Visit Hal Leonard Online at
www.halleonard.com

Contact us:
Hal Leonard
7777 West Bluemound Road
Milwaukee, WI 53213
Email: info@halleonard.com

In Europe, contact:
Hal Leonard Europe Limited
42 Wigmore Street
Marylebone, London, W1U 2RN
Email: info@halleonardeurope.com

In Australia, contact:
Hal Leonard Australia Pty. Ltd.
4 Lentara Court
Cheltenham, Victoria, 3192 Australia
Email: info@halleonard.com.au

CONTENTS

I Want Love

Words and Music by
Elton John and Bernie Taupin

Intro

‖: A F#m | C#m | C D :‖

Verse 1

A   F#m | E | C#m
I want love but it's im - possible.

　　　　F#m | D | C#7
A man like me, so irre - sponsible.

　　　　　| F#m | Bsus4
A man like me is dead in places

　　　B | Bm7 E7sus4 E7
Other men feel liber - ated.

Verse 2

‖ A   F#m | E | C#m
And I can't love shot full of holes.

　　　F#m | D | C#7
Don't feel nothin', I just feel cold.

　　　　　| F#m | Bsus4
Don't feel nothin', just old scars

　　　B | Bm7   E7sus4 E7
Toughening up a - round my heart.

Chorus 1

```
       ‖A          |G/A                    |
But  I want love,    just a diff'rent kind.
D                G9
I want love, won't break me down,
      |A/C♯                F♯7
Won't brick me up, won't fence me in.
        |Bm7
I want a love that don't mean a thing.
           |E7sus4      E7   |C     D       ‖
That's the love I want. I want love.
```

Verse 3

```
A      F♯m  |E                |C♯m
I want love on my own terms,
       F♯m            |D             |C♯7
After ev'rything I've ever learned.
          |F♯m                |Bsus4
Me, I carry too much baggage.
                B  |Bm7     E7sus4  E7
Oh man, I've seen so much traffic.
```

Chorus 2

```
       ‖A          |G/A                    |
But  I want love,    just a diff'rent kind.
D                G9
I want love, won't break me down,
      |A/C♯                F♯7
Won't break me up, won't fence me in.
        |Bm7
I want a love that don't mean a thing.
           |E7sus4      E7   |C     D  C/E ‖
That's the love I want. I want love.
```

Bridge

```
F              |C/E              |G
    So bring it on, I've been bruised.
                            |C    F    C      |Cm
Don't give me love that's clean and smooth.
                    |B♭            |F/A
I'm ready for the rougher stuff.
                    |D/F♯              E7/G♯ ‖
No sweet romance,     I've had enough.
```

Guitar Solo

```
|A    F♯m  |E        |C♯m  F♯m  |D          ‖
```

Pre-Chorus

```
C♯7              F♯m        |Bsus4
   A man like me is dead in places
        B    |Bm7  E7sus4  E7
Other men feel liber - ated.
```

Chorus 3

Repeat Chorus 1

Chorus 4

```
A          |G/A                  |
I want love,    just a diff'rent kind.
D              G9
I want love, won't break me down,
      |A/C♯                F♯7
Won't break me up, won't fence me in.
        |Bm7
I want a love that don't mean a thing.
          |E7sus4    E7   |C    D    ‖
That's the love I want. I want love.
```

Outro

```
|A   F♯m  |C♯m      |C    D   |A          ‖
```

The Bitch Is Back

Words and Music by
Elton John and Bernie Taupin

Tune down 1/2 step:
(low to high) Eb - Ab - Db - Gb - Bb - Eb

A   D/A   E   G   D   F#m

Intro

| A | D/A | A | D/A |
| A | D/A | A | D/A

Verse 1

||A | | | |E A
I was justified when I was five, raising cane, I spit in your eye.
|G |D
The times are changing, now the poor get fat.
|A |E A ||
But the fever's gonna catch you when the bitch gets back, oh.

Interlude 1

|A D/A A D/A | A D/A A |
| D/A A D/A | A D/A ||

Verse 2

A | | |E A
Eat meat on a Friday, that's alright. I even like steak on a Saturday night.
|G |D
I can bitch the best at your so - cial do's,
|A |E A ||
I get high in the evening sniffing pots of glue, ooh.

Interlude 2

|A D/A A D/A | A D/A A

Chorus 1

‖**E** |
I'm a bitch, I'm a bitch, oh, the bitch is back.
|**F♯m**　　　　　|**D**
Stone cold sober as a matter of fact.
|**E** |
I can bitch, I can bitch 'cause I'm better than you.
|**G**　　　　　　|**E**　　　　　　　　‖
It's the way that I move; the things that I do, whoa.

Interlude 3

|**A**　　　　|　**D/A**　|**A**　　　　|　**D/A**　|
|**A**　　　　|　**D/A**　|**A**　　　　|　**D/A**

Verse 3

‖**A**　　　|　　　　|　　　　　　|**E**　　**A**
I entertain by picking brains, sell my soul by dropping names.
|**G**　　　　　　|**D**
I don't like those. My God, what's that?
|**A**　　　　　　|**E**　　**A**　　　‖
Oh, it's full of nasty habits when the bitch gets back, oh.

Interlude 4

|**A**　**D/A**　**A**　**D/A**　|　　　**A**　**D/A**　**A**

Chorus 2

Repeat Chorus 1

Interlude 5

|**A**　　　　|　**D/A**　|**A**　　　　|　**D/A**　‖

Sax Solo

|**A**　　　|　　　|　　　　　|**E**　**A**　|
|**G**　　　|**D**　　|**A**　　　|**E**　**A**　|
|　　**D/A**　**A**　**D/A**　|　　**A**　**D/A**　**A**

Chorus 3

Repeat Chorus 1

Interlude 6

|**A**　　　|　**D/A**　|**A**　　　|　**D/A**　‖

Outro

‖:**A**　　　|**G**　**D**　|**A**　　　|**G**　**D**　:‖
Bitch, bitch,　　　the bitch is back.

Saturday Night's Alright (For Fighting)

Words and Music by
Elton John and Bernie Taupin

D5 G5 C5 F5 G5* C5* G F C

Dm7 B♭ E♭ B♭* Csus4 C* D5* F5*

Intro

D5 G5 D5	G5 D5 G5
C5 F5 C5	G5* C5* G5* C5*
D5 G5 D5	G5 D5 G5
C5 F5 C5	G5* C5* G5* C5*

Verse 1

‖G |
It's getting late, have you seen my mates?
|F |
Ma, tell me when the boys get here.
|C |
It's seven o'clock and I wanna rock,
|G |
Wanna get a belly full of beer.
| |
My old man's drunker than a barrel full of monkeys
|F |
And my old lady, she don't care.
|C |
My sister looks cute in her braces and boots,
|G |Dm7 |
A handful of grease in her hair.

Chorus 1

```
            ‖C                    |
```
Oh, don't give us none of your aggravation,
```
       |Bb                   |
```
We've had it with your discipline.
```
     |F                    |
```
Oh, Saturday night's alright for fightin',
```
        |C                 |
```
Get ___ a little action in.
```
     |                     |
```
Get about as oiled as a diesel train.
```
       |Bb                 |
```
Gonna set this dance alight.
```
         |F                  |
```
'Cause Saturday night's the night I like.
```
     |C           |              |G
```
Saturday night's alright, alright, alright.
```
Eb  Bb*  Eb  Bb*  |Csus4   C*    |          |
```
Oo. _____
```
G   |D5*    F5*    G    |           |D5*    F5*    G    |
```


Verse 2

```
            ‖G                    |
```
Well, they're packed pretty tight in here tonight.
```
     |F                    |
```
I'm lookin' for a dolly to see me right.
```
        |C                      |
```
I may use a little muscle to get what I need.
```
        |G                      |
```
I may sink a little drink and shout out "She's with me!"
```
     |                    |
```
A couple of the sounds that I really like
```
         |F                       |
```
Are the sounds of a switchblade and a motor bike.
```
        |C                  |
```
I'm a juvenile product of the working class
```
          |G                      |
```
Whose best friend floats in the bottom of a glass.

Chorus 2

    |**Dm7** | ‖**C** |
Oh, _____   don't give us none of your aggravation,

     |**B♭** |
We've had it with your discipline.

F |
Saturday night's alright for fightin',

    |**C** |
Get ___ a little action in.

    | |
Get about as oiled as a diesel train.

    |**B♭** |
Gonna set this dance alight.

      |**F** |
'Cause Saturday night's the night I like.

   |**C** | |**G** |
Saturday night's alright, alright, alright.

E♭ **B♭*** **E♭** **B♭*** |**Csus4**   **C*** | ‖
Oo. _____

Interlude 1

    ‖:**C** | |**B♭** | |
    |**F** | |**C** | :‖

Chorus 3

Dm7 ‖ C |

    Oh,   don't give us none of your aggravation,

   |B♭ |

We've had it with your discipline.

F |

Saturday night's alright for fightin',

   |C |

Get ____ a little action in.

   | |

 Get about as oiled as a diesel train.

    |B♭ |

Gonna set this dance alight.

    |F |

'Cause Saturday night's the night I like.

  |C | |G |

Saturday night's alright, alright, alright.

E♭ B♭* E♭ B♭* |Csus4   C* | ‖

Oo. _____

Interlude 2

|C | |B♭ | |

|F | |C | ‖

Outro

‖: C | |

    Saturday, Saturday, Saturday,

B♭ | |

Saturday, Saturday, Saturday,

F | |C | :‖

Saturday, Saturday, Saturday night's alright.   *Play 3 times*

‖: C | |B♭ | |

|F | |C | :‖   *Repeat and fade*

Thank You for All Your Loving

Words and Music by
Elton John and Caleb Quaye

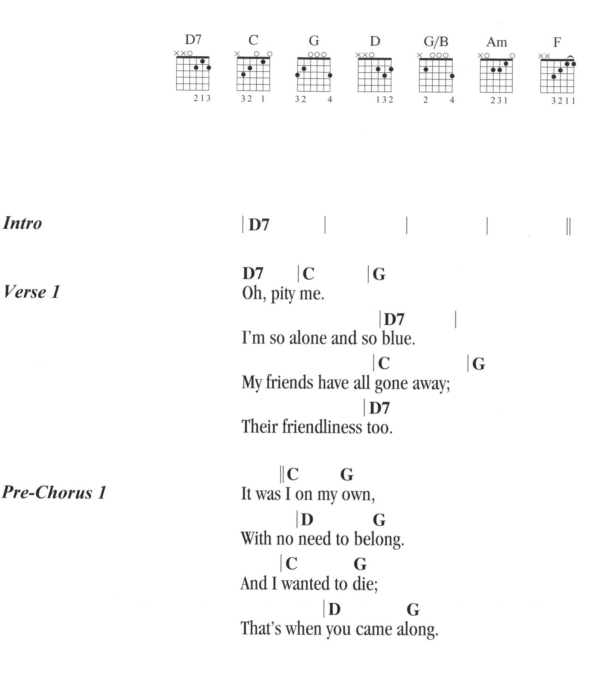

Intro | **D7** | | | ‖

Verse 1

D7 |**C** |**G**
Oh, pity me.

              |**D7** |
I'm so alone and so blue.

           |**C** |**G**
My friends have all gone away;

           |**D7**
Their friendliness too.

Pre-Chorus 1

     ‖**C**   **G**
It was I on my own,

     |**D**   **G**
With no need to belong.

    |**C**   **G**
And I wanted to die;

     |**D**   **G**
That's when you came along.

Chorus 1	‖ **C** **G/B Am** |**G** | And thank you for all of your loving. **C** **G/B Am** |**G** | Thank you for all of your tears. **C** **G/B Am** |**G** | Thank you for all of your kindness. **F** **C** |**G** ‖ Thank you for being here.
Interlude 1	| **D7** | | | ‖

Verse 2	**D7** |**C** |**G**
	   What a diff'rence it made,
	         |**D7** |
	My life done started again.
	      |**C** |**G**
	And if you go away,
	       |**D7** ‖
	It just won't be the same.

Pre-Chorus 2	**C** **G**
	   It's hard to say
	   |**D** **G**
	What I feel when I'm by your side.
	   |**C** **G**
	You're there when I'm worried;
	   |**D** **G**
	All my troubles in you I confide.

Chorus 2	*Repeat Chorus 1*
Interlude 2	*Repeat Interlude 1*
Verse 3	*Repeat Verse 1*
Pre-Chorus 3	*Repeat Pre-Chorus 1*
Chorus 3	*Repeat Chorus 1*
Interlude 3	*Repeat Interlude 1*
Outro	‖: **D7** | :‖ ***Repeat and fade***

Border Song

Words and Music by
Elton John and Bernie Taupin

C　　F/C　　G/B　　Am　　E7　　Esus4　　E　　F

Dm　　F#°7　　C/G　　F/G　　C/E　　D7/F#　　Gsus4

Intro　　|C　　F/C　C　F/C |C　　F/C　C　G/B ||

Verse 1

Am　　E7　|Am　E7　Am　　|
　Holy Moses,　I have been removed.

C　　　　　　　　G/B |C　　　　　　Esus4　E |C
I have seen the specter;　he has been here too.

　　　　　　　　　　　　　　　　G/B　　　　　|F
Distant cousin from down the line,

　　　　　　　　　　　　Dm　　　　　　|
Brand of people who ain't my kind.

F　F#°7 |C/G　F/G　　　　　　|C　F/C　C　　F/C |C　F/C　C　　G/B ||
Ho - ly　　Moses, I have been removed.

Verse 2

Am　　E7　|Am　E7　Am　　|
　Holy Moses,　I have been deceived.

C　　　　　　　　G/B　　　|C　　　　　　Esus4　E |C
Now the wind has changed direction and I'll have to leave.

　　　　　　　G/B　　　　　　　　　　|F　　　　　　Dm　　　|
Won't you please excuse my frankness, but it's not my cup of tea.

F　F#°7 |C/G　F/G　　　　　　|C　F/C　C　　F/C |C　F/C　C
Ho - ly　　Moses, I have been deceived.

Bridge

```
     ‖C          C/E          F
```
I'm goin' back to the border where my affairs,

```
     |C      F/G    C          |
```
Where my affairs ain't a - bused.

```
        C/E        F
```
I can't take any more bad water;

```
     |D7/F♯                    |Gsus4
```
Been poisoned from my head down to my shoes.

```
   |C   F/C   C   F/C |C   F/C   C   G/B‖
```
Oh.

Interlude

```
|Am  E7  |Am  E7  Am    |C   G/B |C     Esus4  E |
|C   G/B |F        Dm       |
F   F♯°7 |C/G   F/G          |C    F/C   C    F/C |C    F/C   C     G/B   ‖
```
Ho - ly   Moses, I have been deceived.

Verse 3

```
Am       E7  |Am   E7   Am      |C
```
   Holy Moses,   let us live in peace.

```
            G/B        |C          Esus4   E |C
```
Let us strive to find a way to make all hatred cease.

```
            G/B        |F              Dm        |
```
There's a man o - ver there.   What's his color? I don't care.

```
F   F♯°7 |C/G   F/G          |C
```
He's my   brother. Let us live in peace.

```
C/E  F   F♯°7 |C/G   F/G          |C
```
Oh, he's my   brother. Let us live in peace.

```
C/E  F   F♯°7 |C/G   F/G              |C  F/C  C  F/C |C  F/C  C    ‖
```
Oh, he's my   brother. Let us, let us live in peace.

Rock and Roll Madonna

Words and Music by
Elton John and Bernie Taupin

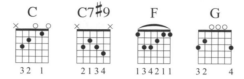

Intro

|C | |C7♯9 | |
| | | | |

Verse 1

‖C | |F |
If anyone should see me makin' it down the highway,
|C | |G |
Breakin' all the laws of the land,
|C | |F |
Well, don't you try to stop me, I'm goin' her way.
|C |G |C |
And that's the way I'm sure she had it planned.

Chorus 1

‖C | |F |
Well, that's my Rock and Roll Madonna.
|C | |G |
She's always been a lady of the road.
|C | |F |
Well ev'rybody wants her, but no one ever gets her.
|C |G |C |
The freeway is the only way she knows.

Verse 2

```
                  ‖ C              |                        |F         |
Well, if she would only slow down for a short time,
   |C              |                   |G            |
I'd get to know her just before she leaves.
              |C              |          |F                    |
But she's got some fascination for that two wheel combination,
              |C          |G          |C          |
And I swear it's gonna be the death of me.
```

Chorus 2   *Repeat Chorus 1*

Piano Solo   *Repeat Verse 1 (Instrumental)*

Interlude   ‖: C7#9 | :‖

                      | |

Chorus 3   *Repeat Chorus 1*

Breakdown

```
|C          |          |F          |          |
|C          |          |G          |          |
|C          |          |F          |          |
|C          |G         |C          |
```

Chorus 4

```
                  ‖ C              |                  |F         |
Well, that's my Rock and Roll Madonna.
         |C              |              |G          |
She's always been a lady of the road.
         |C          |          |F          |
Well ev'rybody wants her, but no one ever gets her.
         |C          |G          |C          |              ‖
The freeway is the only way she knows.
```

Your Song

Words and Music by
Elton John and Bernie Taupin

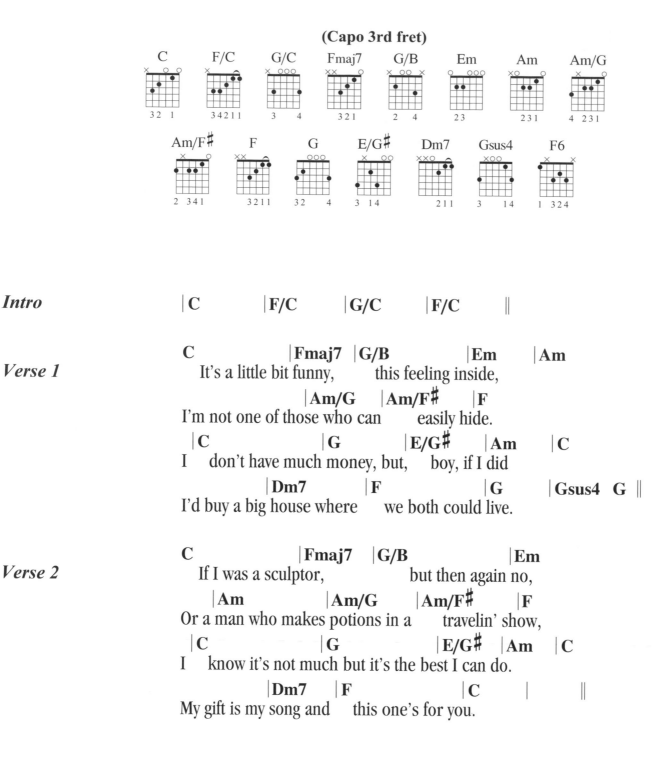

(Capo 3rd fret)

Intro |C |F/C |G/C |F/C ||

Verse 1

C |Fmaj7 |G/B |Em |Am
It's a little bit funny,   this feeling inside,
                              |Am/G |Am/F# |F
I'm not one of those who can   easily hide.
   |C |G |E/G# |Am |C
I   don't have much money, but,   boy, if I did
                    |Dm7 |F |G |Gsus4   G ||
I'd buy a big house where   we both could live.

Verse 2

C |Fmaj7 |G/B |Em
If I was a sculptor,   but then again no,
      |Am |Am/G |Am/F# |F
Or a man who makes potions in a   travelin' show,
   |C |G |E/G# |Am |C
I   know it's not much but it's the best I can do.
                    |Dm7 |F |C | ||
My gift is my song and   this one's for you.

Chorus 1

```
        G/B              |Am       |Dm7            |F         |G/B
     And you can tell ev'rybody    this is your song.
                 |Am        |Dm7           |F          |Am
     It may be quite simple but,      now that it's done,
                            |Am/G                      |Am/F♯
     I hope you don't mind,        I hope you don't mind
                        |F6          |
     That I put down in words
         |C         |F        |            |G         |Gsus4   G  ‖
     How wonderful life is while you're in the world.
```

Interlude

```
 |C          |F/C       |G/C       |F/C          ‖
```

Verse 3

```
     C               |Fmaj7  |G/B              |Em
      I sat on the roof        and kicked off the moss.
             |Am        |Am/G           |Am/F♯      |F        |C
     Well, a few    of the verses, well, they've got me quite cross.
                        |G      |E/G♯               |Am       |C
     But the sun's been quite kind      while I wrote this song.
                           |Dm7   |F              |G        |Gsus4   G  ‖
     It's for people like you that     keep it turned on.
```

Verse 4

```
     C               |Fmaj7  |G/B              |Em        |Am
      So excuse me forgetting,        but these things I do.
                  |Am/G         |Am/F♯         |F          |C
     You see, I've forgotten if they're green or they're blue.
                        |G             |E/G♯   |Am      |C
     Anyway, the thing is    what I really mean,
                        |Dm7   |F            |C         |        ‖
     Yours are the sweetest eyes     I've ever seen.
```

Chorus 2

Repeat Chorus 1

Outro

```
     Am                        |Am/G                      |Am/F♯
      I hope you don't mind,        I hope you don't mind
                      |F6          |
     That I put down in words
         |C         |F        |            |C        |F/C   |G/C   |F/C   |C      ‖
     How wonderful life is while you're in the world.
```

Amoreena

Words and Music by
Elton John and Bernie Taupin

G   F   C/E   G7(no3rd)   D   A/C#   C   Dm7   Bm

Em   B°7   Esus4   E   Am   C/G   Fm7   D7sus4   D7

Intro

G	F	C/E	G G7(no3rd) C/E
G	F	C/E	G
D	A/C#	C	G
D	A/C#	C	G
G7(no3rd) C/E ‖

Verse 1

G |F |C/E
Lately I've been thinking
      Dm7 |G
How much I miss my lady.
   |Bm |Em   Dm7 |C
Amoreena's in a cornfield
         |G |
Brightening the daybreak,
         |F |C/E
Living like a lusty flow'r.
   Dm7 |G |
Running through the grass for hours,
Bm |Em   Dm7 |C
Rolling through the hay,
         |G   ‖
Like a puppy child.

Chorus 1

D |A/C# |C
And when it rains, the rain falls down,
                    |G |D
Washing out the cattle town.
                    |A/C# |C
And she's far away somewhere
         |G |B°7
In her eiderdown;
                    |Esus4   E
And she dreams of crystal streams,
  |Am   C/G |F |
Of days gone by when we would lean,
Fm7 | |D7sus4 |D7
Laughing, fit to burst upon each other.

Verse 2

    ‖G |F |C/E
I can see you sitting, eating
Dm7 |G
Apples in the evening,
  |Bm |Em   Dm7
The fruit juice flowing slowly, slowly,
  |C |G |
Slowly down the bronze of your body;
        |F |C/E
Living like a lusty flow'r,
  Dm7 |G |
Running through the grass for hours,
Bm |Em Dm7 |C
Rolling through the hay,   whoa,
         |G   ‖
Like a puppy child.

Chorus 2   *Repeat Chorus 1*

‖ **G**   **|F**   **|C/E**
Oh, if only I could nestle

     Dm7   **|G**
In the cradle of your cabin,

 |Bm   **|Em**
My arms around your shoulder,

Dm7   **|C**   **|G**
Whoa, the windows wide and open

         | **|F**   **|C/E**
While the swallow and the sycamore

     Dm7   **|G**
Are playing in the valley.

 |Bm   **|Em**
Oh, I miss you, Amoreena,

Dm7 **|C**   **|G**   ‖
Like the king bee misses honey.

Chorus 3

D   **|A/C♯**   **|C**
    And when it rains, the rain falls down,

            |G   **|D**
Washing out the cattle town.

        |A/C♯   **|C**
And she's far away somewhere

     |G   **|B°7**
In her eiderdown;

              |Esus4 **E**
And she dreams of crystal streams,

 |Am   **C/G**   **|F** |
Of days gone by when we would lean,

Fm7 | **|G** | ‖
Laughing, fit to burst upon each other.

Chorus 4   *Repeat Chorus 1*

Interlude ‖: G |F |C/E |G G7(no3rd) C/E :‖

Verse 4

G |F |C/E
Lately I've been thinking

     Dm7 |G
How much I miss my lady.

 |Bm |Em Dm7 |C
Amoreena's in a cornfield

      |G |
Brightening the daybreak,

     |F |C/E
Living like a lusty flow'r.

 Dm7 |G |
Running through the grass for hours,

Bm |Em Dm7 |C
Rolling through the hay,

    | |G |G7(no3rd) C/E |G ‖
Like a puppy, like a puppy child.

Crocodile Rock

Words and Music by
Elton John and Bernie Taupin

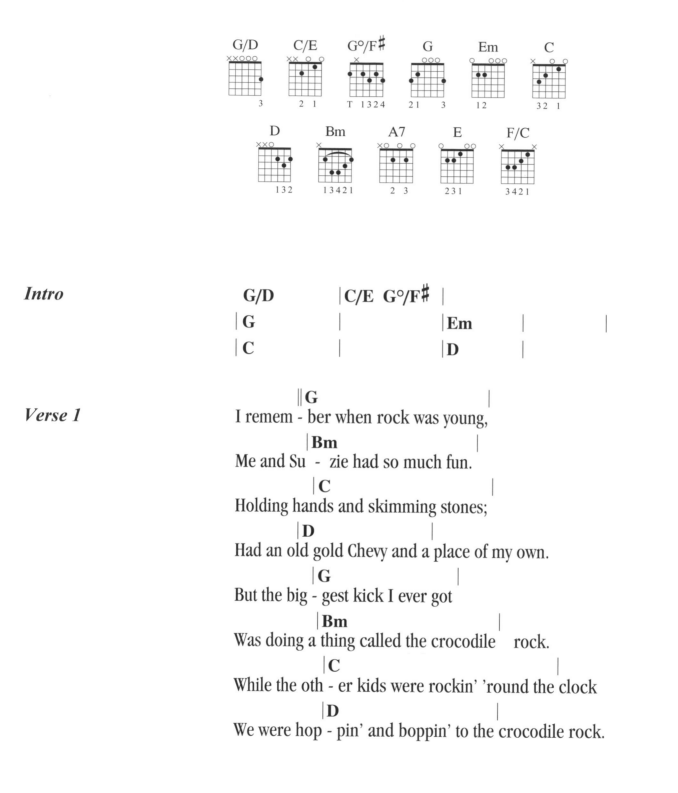

Intro

G/D		C/E G°/F♯
G	|Em	
C		D

Verse 1

‖G |
I remem - ber when rock was young,

|Bm |
Me and Su - zie had so much fun.

|C |
Holding hands and skimming stones;

|D |
Had an old gold Chevy and a place of my own.

|G |
But the big - gest kick I ever got

|Bm |
Was doing a thing called the crocodile rock.

|C |
While the oth - er kids were rockin' 'round the clock

|D |
We were hop - pin' and boppin' to the crocodile rock.

Chorus 1

‖**Em** |
Well,   crocodile rockin' is something shockin'

|**A7** | |**D**
When your feet just can't keep still.

| |**G** |
I never knew me a better time and I guess I never will.

|**E** |
Oh, Lawdy Mama, those Friday nights

|**A7** |
When Suzie wore her dresses tight

|**D** |**F/C**   C   F/C | C   F/C   C ‖
And   the crocodile rockin' was out of sight.

Interlude 1

G | |**Em** |
La,   la, la, la, la, la.

|**C** | |**D** |
La, la, la, la,la.   La, la, la, la, la.

Verse 2

‖**G** |
But the years went by and rock just died,

|**Bm** |
Su - zie went and left us for some foreign guy.

|**C** |
Long nights cryin' by the record machine,

|**D** |
Dream - in' of my Chevy and my old blue jeans.

|**G** |
But they'll never kill the thrills we got

|**Bm** |
Burnin' up to the crocodile rock

|**C** |
Learning fast as the weeks went past;

|**D** |
We really thought the crocodile rock would last.

Chorus 2   *Repeat Chorus 1*

Interlude 2   *Repeat Interlude 1*

Verse 3   *Repeat Verse 1*

Chorus 3   *Repeat Chorus 1*

Outro

‖: **G** | |**Em** |
  La,   la, la, la, la, la.

|**C** | |**D** | :‖
La, la, la, la,la.   La, la, la, la, la.   *Repeat and fade*

25

Tiny Dancer

Words and Music by
Elton John and Bernie Taupin

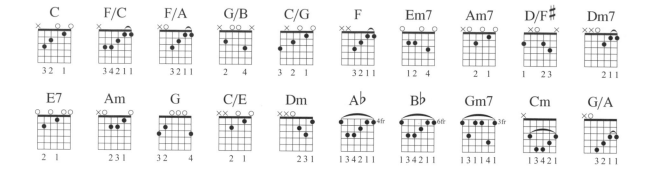

Intro ‖: C   F/C | C   F/C :‖

Verse 1

   C   F/C |C   F/C |C
   Blue jean baby,   L.A. lady,
                |F/A   G/B |C
Seamstress for the band.
       F/C |C   F/C |C
Pretty eyed,   pirate smile,
              |F/A   C/G |F
You'll marry a music man.
     Em7 |Am7   D/F# |Dm7
Balleri - na,   you must have seen her
E7 |Am G/B |C
Dancing in the sand.
        F/C |C   F/C |C
And now she's in me, always with me,
               |G F C/E Dm ‖
Tiny dancer in my hand.

Interlude 1 |C   F/C |C   F/C   ‖

       C   F/C |C   F/C |C

Verse 2   Jesus freaks   out in the street

                     |F/A   G/B |C

Handing tickets out for God.

        F/C |C   F/C |C

Turning back,   she just laughs;

                 |F/A   C/G |F

The boulevard is not that bad.

     Em7 |Am7   D/F♯ |Dm7

Piano man,   he makes his stand

    E7 |Am   G |C

In the auditorium.

       F/C |C   F/C |C

Looking on   she sings the songs.

                 |G   F C/E Dm ‖

The words she knows, the tune she hums.

Interlude 2 |C   F/C |C   ‖

Pre-Chorus 1

  A♭   B♭ |
   But oh, how it feels so real

Gm7   **Cm**
Lying here with no one near.

  |**A♭** |**B♭**
On - ly you, and you can hear me

          |**G/B**| ||
When I say softly, slowly…

Chorus 1

‖:**F**   **C/E** |**Dm** |**F**
   Hold me clos - er, Tiny Dancer;

            C/E |**G/A** |**F**
Count the headlights on the highway.

       C/E |**Dm** |**F**
Lay me down in sheets of linen;

        C/E |**G/A**   :‖
You had a busy day today.

Interlude 3 |**F/A** |**G/A** |**F/C** |**C** **F/C** |**C** **F/C** ‖

Verse 3   *Repeat Verse 1*

Interlude 4   *Repeat Interlude 2*

Pre-Chorus 2   *Repeat Pre-Chorus 1*

Chorus 2   *Repeat Chorus 1*

Outro |**F/A** |**C** **F/C** |**C** **F/C** |**C** **F/C** |**C** **F/C** **C** ‖

Take Me to the Pilot

Words and Music by
Elton John and Bernie Taupin

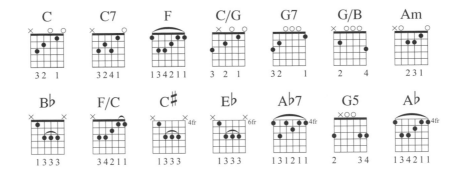

Intro |C   C7 |F |C/G G7 |C

Verse 1
              ‖C |
If ya feel that it's real,

G/B |Am
I'm on trial

            |B♭   F |C |F/C
And I'm here in your prison.

            |C |
Like a coin in your mint

G/B |Am
I am, dented

            |B♭   F |C | C#   ‖
And I'm spent with high treason.

Pre-Chorus 1

```
Eb                      |          |F
    Through a glass eye your throne
                 |          |
    Is the one danger zone.
Ab7            |          |G5        |          |
Take me to the pilot for control.
C       Bb     |Ab  Eb     |C         |
Take me to the pilot  of your soul.
```

Chorus 1

```
    F/C          ‖C     C7              |F
    Take me to the pilot; lead me through the chamber.
                 |C/G  G7      |C
    Take me to the pilot; I am but a stranger.
                 |      C7              |F
    Take me to the pilot; lead me through the chamber.
                 |C/G  G7      |C
    Take me to the pilot; I am but a stranger.
             |    C7      |F        |C/G
    Na, na, na,     na, na, na, na, na, na,
         G7      |C
    Na, na, na, na, na.
             |    C7      |F        |C/G
    Na, na, na,     na, na, na, na, na, na,
         G7      |C          ‖
    Na, na, na, na, na.
```

Breakdown 1

```
|C7   F  |C    F   |C7  F  |          |
|C         |
```

Verse 2

```
F/C          ‖C          |      |Am
    Well, I know he's not old,
             |Bb         F     |C          |F/C
And I'm told, and I'm told he's a virgin.
     |C          |
Or he may be she.
             |Am
What I'm told,
         |Bb       F    |C      |F/C    C ‖
And I'm never, never for certain.
```

Pre-Chorus 2   *Repeat Pre-Chorus 1*

Chorus 2   *Repeat Chorus 1*

Breakdown 2	|C7 F |C F |C7 F	
	|C	F/C ‖

Interlude

|C | |Am |B♭ F |
|C | | | |
|Am |B♭ F |C |F/C   ‖

Pre-Chorus 3

Repeat Pre-Chorus 1

Chorus 3

                ‖C   C7 |F
Take me to the pilot; lead me through the chamber.
               |C/G G7 |C
Take me to the pilot; I am but a stranger.
          | C7 |F
Take me to the pilot; lead me through the chamber.
               |C/G G7 |C
Take me to the pilot; I am but a stranger.

Outro

‖:   ‖C C7 |F
  Na, na, na, na, na, na,
         |C/G G7 |C
Na, na, na, na, na, na, na, na.
      | C7 |F
Na, na, na,   na, na, na,
       |C/G G7 |C   :‖
Na, na, na, na, na, na, na, na.   ***Repeat and fade***

Hercules

Words and Music by
Elton John and Bernie Taupin

Intro

G C/G G |
| C/G G C/G G | C/G G C/G G |
| C/G G C/G G | ‖

Verse 1

G | |
    Ooh, I got a busted wing and a hornet sting,
  | |C
Like an out of tune guitar.
    F | C F | C F | C G/B |Am
    | G/B |C
Ooh, she got Hercules on her   side,
  | |G
And Diana in her eyes.
    C | G C | G C | G |
    | |
Some men like the Chinese life;
  | |C
Some men need a break.
    F | C F | C F | C G/B |Am
    | G/B |C
Oo, well, I like women, and I   like wine,
  | |G | |
And I've always liked it that way.
F C/E Dm   C |G |
Al - ways liked it that way.
    |
(Do wop, shoo op.
    | ‖
Do wop, shoo op. Do wop, shoo op. Ah.)

Chorus 1

```
D             |G
  I can't dig it,
              |            |D
The way she tease;
              |            |G
That old tough man routine
              |
Up her sleeve.
 |C              |D
Living and loving, kissing and hugging,
 |Em             |C          |G           |
Living and loving with a cat named Hercules.
 |F  C/E   Dm   C ||
A cat named Hercules.
```

Interlude 1

```
|G  C/G  G   C/G  G|  C/G  G   C/G  G|
|           C/G        G|  C/G                ||
```

Verse 2

```
G         |
  Oh, and it hurts like hell
  |        |            |C
To see my gal messing with a muscle boy.
   F|  C  F|  C  F|  C  G/B|Am
      |              G/B|C        |
No Superman gonna ruin my    plans,
              |G
Playing with my toys.
   C|  G  C|  G  C|  G    |
        |            |
Rich man sweating in a sauna bath;
      |            |C
Poor boy   scrubbing in a tub.
   F|  C  F|  C  F|  C  G/B|Am
      |          G/B |C
Me, I stay gritty up to my    ears,
   |                |G      |      |
Washing in a bucket of mud.
F       C/E Dm   C  |G        |
Washing in a   bucket of mud.
                       |
(Do wop, shoo op.
                   |        ||
Do wop, shoo op. Do wop, shoo op. Ah.)
```

Chorus 2   *Repeat Chorus 1*

Interlude 2   *Repeat Interlude 1*

Guitar Solo   *Repeat Verse 1 (Instrumental)*

Chorus 3

D | | G
   But I can't dig it,

            | | D
The way she tease;

            | | G
That old tough man routine

        |
Up her sleeve.

 | C | D
Living and loving, kissing and hugging,

 | Em | C | G |
Living and loving with a cat named Hercules.

 | F C/E   Dm   C | G C/G G   C/G G | C/G G
A cat named Hercules.

 | F C/E   Dm   C | G C/G G   C/G G | C/G G
A cat named Hercules.

 | F C/E   Dm   C | G C/G G   C/G G | C/G G
A cat named Hercules.

 | F C/E   Dm   C ‖
A cat named Hercules.

Outro   ‖: G | :‖ *Repeat and fade*

Don't Go Breaking My Heart

Words and Music by
Carte Blanche and Ann Orson

F	Dm	Bb	C	A7	G7/B	F/C

1 3 4 2 1 1   2 3 1   1 3 3 3   3 2   1   2   3   2   1   3 4 2 1 1

Bb*	Am	Cm7	G	Ab	C7

3 3 3   2 3 1   1 3 1 2 1   3 2   4   1 3 4 2 1 1   3 2 4 1

Intro
```
|F    Dm|       Bb|    C  F|          Bb|
|      F|       Bb|          ||
```

Verse 1
```
 F                    |Bb      |F
    Don't go breaking my heart.
                   |Bb      |F
I couldn't if I tried.
    A7        |Bb   G7/B  |F/C
Oh, honey, if I    get restless,
                 |Bb   F  Bb*|   F   Bb* C ||
Baby, you're not that kind.
```

Verse 2
```
 F                    |Bb      |F
    Don't go breaking my heart.
                  |Bb       |F
You take the weight off of me.
    A7         |Bb          G7/B  |F/C
Oh, honey, when you knock on my door,
                 |Bb  F  Bb*|   F   Bb*     ||
Oo, I gave you my key.
```

Chorus 1

```
          Am    |          |Cm7        |
          Oo, oo, nobody knows it,
            |Bb        F    |C       G      |
          But when I was down, I was your clown.
          Am    |          |Cm7               |
          Oo, oo, nobody knows it, nobody knows it.
            |Bb        F    |C       G      |
          But right from the start I gave you my heart.
          Ab   |C                |Bb  F  Bb* | F  Bb* C | F
          Oh, oh,      I gave you my heart.
                                    |Dm        |Bb
          So, don't go breaking my heart.
                    C              |F   C  Dm |      C  Bb |
          I won't go breaking your heart.
                        C          |F    Bb|     F|     Bb|        ||
          Don't go breaking my heart.
```

Verse 3

```
          F            |Bb        |F
            Nobody told us.
                             |Bb        |F
          'Cause nobody showed us.
          A7         |Bb  G7/B    |F/C
          Now it's up to us, babe.
                                |Bb   F   Bb* |   F   Bb* C  ||
          Whoa, I think we can make it.
```

Verse 4

```
          F                    |Bb          |F
            So don't misunderstand me.
                               |Bb          |F
          You put the light in my life.
                    A7         |Bb      G7/B   |F/C
          Oh, you put the spark to the flame.
                                 |Bb   F   Bb* |  F   Bb*      ||
          I've got your heart in my sights.
```

Chorus 2   *Repeat Chorus 1*

Interlude

```
|F        |B♭       |F        |B♭        |
|F    A7  |B♭  G7/B |F/C   B♭|   F  B♭*|              ||
```

Chorus 3

```
 Am    |            |Cm7       |
Oo, oo, nobody knows it,
  |B♭       F  |C        G
But when I was down, I was your clown.
  |B♭        F  |C          G    |
But right from the start I gave you my heart.
A♭  |C                    |B♭   F   B♭* |F  B♭*  C  ||
Oh, oh,       I gave you my heart.
```

Outro

```
F                          |Dm        |B♭
  So, don't go breaking my heart.
        C            |F
I won't go breaking your heart.
               |Dm                |B♭
Don't go breaking my,    don't go breaking my,
        C        |F
Don't go breaking my heart.
               |Dm                  |B♭
Don't go breaking my,    don't go breaking my,
        C            |F
I won't go breaking your heart.
               |Dm                   B♭
Don't go breaking my heart. Don't go breaking my,
        C            |F
I won't go breaking your heart.
               |Dm                   B♭
Don't go breaking my heart. Don't go breaking my,
        C            |F            ||
I won't go breaking your heart.
```

Honky Cat

Words and Music by
Elton John and Bernie Taupin

D7   G   B7   E7

Intro

| D7 | | | |
| G | | | ||

Verse 1

D7 | | | | G
When I look back, boy, I must have been green

| | | | D7
Boppin' in the country, fishin' in a stream.

| | | | G
Lookin' for an answer, tryin' to find a sign.

| | | |
Until I saw your city lights, honey, I was blind.

Chorus 1

|| B7 | | |
They said,   get back, honky cat, better get back to the woods.

| E7 | | | | D7
Well, I   quit those days and my redneck ways and a,

| | | | G | | |
Hmm, hmm, hmm, hmm, oh, the change is gonna do me good.

Chorus 2

|| B7 | | |
You better   get back, honky cat, livin' in the city ain't where it's at.

| E7 | | |
It's like   tryin' to find gold in a silver mine.

| D7 | | | | G | | |
It's like   tryin' to drink whiskey, oh, from a bottle of wine.

Verse 2

|| D7 | | |
Well, I   read some books and I read some magazines

| G | | |
About those   high class ladies down in New Orleans.

| D7 | | |
And all the   folks back home, well, they said I was a fool.

| G | | |
They said,   oh, believe in the Lord is the golden rule.

Chorus 3

‖ **B7** | | |

They said,   get back, honky cat, better get back to the woods.

|**E7** | | | |**D7**

Well, I   quit those days and my redneck ways.

| | | |**G** | | | ‖

Oo, oo, oo, oo, oh, the change is gonna do me good.

Interlude

|**D7** | | | |

|**G** | | | |

|**D7** | | | |

|**G** | | |

Chorus 4

‖ **B7** | | |

They said,   get back, honky cat, better get back to the woods.

|**E7** | | | |**D7**

Well, I   quit those days and my redneck ways.

| | | |**G** | | |

Oo, oo, oo, oo, oh, the change is gonna do me good.

Verse 3

‖ **D7** | | | |**G**

They said,   stay at home, boy, you gotta tend the farm.

| | |

Livin' in the city, boy, is, is gonna break your heart.

|**D7** | | |

But   how can you stay when your heart says no?

|**G** | | |

Ah, ah,   how can you stop when your feet say go?

Chorus 5

‖ **B7** | | |

You better   get back, honky cat, better get back to the woods.

|**E7** | | | |**D7**

Well, I   quit those days and my redneck ways and a,

| | | |**G** | | |

Oo, oo, oo, oo, oh, the change is gonna do me good.

Chorus 6

Repeat Chorus 2

Outro

‖: **D7** | | | |**G** | | | :‖

    Get back, honky cat, get back, honky cat, get back, ooh.

‖: **D7** | | | |

|**G** | | | :‖ *Repeat and fade*

Pinball Wizard

Words and Music by
Peter Townshend

Cm   Bb/C   Gadd4/B   G7/B   Bb6   Ab6   G   Ab/G

F/C   C   Bb   Ab   Gsus4   G*   C*   Eb

F   F*   Bb*   A   D   E   Dm7

Prelude

|Cm |Bb/C |Gadd4/B |G7/B |
(Ah,

|Bb6 |Ab6 |Cm |G |
Ah,   ah,

|Ab/G |G ||
Ah.)

Intro

|F/C |C |F/C |C |
|F/C |C |F/C |C

Verse 1

          ||C |
Ever since I was a young boy I've played the silver ball.
          |Bb |
From Soho down to Brighton, I must have played them all,
          |Ab |
But I ain't seen nothing like him in any amusement hall.
          |Gsus4 |G*
That deaf, dumb and blind kid sure plays a mean pinball.

Interlude 1	`|C* B♭ E♭ F |` `|C* B♭ E♭ F |`

Verse 2

    `‖C`   `|`   `|`
He stands like a statue, becomes part of the machine.
`B♭`   `|`
Feeling all the bumpers, always playing clean,
  `|A♭`   `|`
He plays by intuition; the digit counters fall.
   `|Gsus4`   `|G*`   `‖`
That deaf, dumb and blind kid sure plays a mean pinball.

Interlude 2   *Repeat Interlude 1*

Chorus 1

    `‖F* G* C*`
He's a pin - ball wizard;
      `F*|  G* C*`
There has to be a twist.
 `|F* G* C*`
A pin - ball wizard's
  `|E♭`   `|B♭*`   `|`   `‖`
Got such a supple wrist.

Bridge

  `B♭*`   `A♭  E♭ B♭*|`
(How do you think he does it?)
  `A♭   E♭`   `|`
I don't know.
 `B♭*`   `A♭ E♭ B♭*`   `|`
(What makes him so   good?)

Verse 3

    `‖C`   `|`   `|`
Oh, he ain't got no distractions, can't hear no buzzes and bells.
`B♭`   `|`   `|`
Don't see lights a-flashing; he plays by sense of smell.
`A♭`   `|`
Always has a replay and never tilts at all.
   `|Gsus4`   `|G*`   `‖`
That deaf, dumb and blind kid sure plays a mean pinball.

Interlude 3   *Repeat Interlude 1*

Chorus 2

```
        ‖F*  G*      C*
He can't beat me now;
       F* |     G*      C*
I've al - ways been the champ.
  |F*   G*  C*
I know ev'ry trick;
      |E♭              |B♭*      |        ‖
No freaks gonna beat my hand.
```

Guitar Solo 1

```
‖: B♭*      A♭      |E♭        B♭*      :‖
  (Oh,               get it straight.)          *Play 4 times*
| F/C         |C            |F/C         |C
```

Verse 4

```
      ‖C                 |
Even on my usual table, he can beat the best.
      |B♭                |
His disciples lead him in and he just does the rest.
      |A♭                   |
He's got crazy flipper fingers; I've never seen him fall.
      |Gsus4              |G*                ‖
That deaf, dumb and blind kid sure plays a mean pinball.
```

Interlude 4

```
|C*  B♭  E♭  F  |              |C*  B♭  E♭  F  |              |
|              |              |G*                |
```

Chorus 3

```
      ‖G*  A   D
He's a pin - ball wizard.
       G* |   A   D
There has to be a twist.
 |G*  A   D
A pin - ball wizard's
     |F         |C*      |        |        |
Got such a supple wrist.
```

Chorus 4

‖**G* A   D**
He's a pin - ball wizard.

  G* | **A   D**
He'll score two trillion more.

 |**G* A   D**
A pin - ball wizard,

  |**F** |**C*** |
The world's new pinball lord.

                  |**D** |
He's scoring more.

              |**E** | ‖
He's scoring more.

Guitar Solo 2

‖: **Dm7   G*** | **Dm7   G***   :‖ *Play 7 times*
 |**Dm7   G*** | **Dm7   G*****

Chorus 5

 ‖**G***   **A   D**
I thought I   was

   G*| **A   D**
The Bally table king,

 |**G* A   D**
But I   just handed

 |**F** |**C**‖** |
My pinball crown to him,

 |**D** |
To him,

 |**E** | ‖
To him.

Outro

‖: **C* B♭** |**F   C*** | **B♭** |**F   C*** :‖ *Repeat and fade*

43

Rocket Man
(I Think It's Gonna Be a Long Long Time)

Words and Music by
Elton John and Bernie Taupin

(Capo 3rd fret)

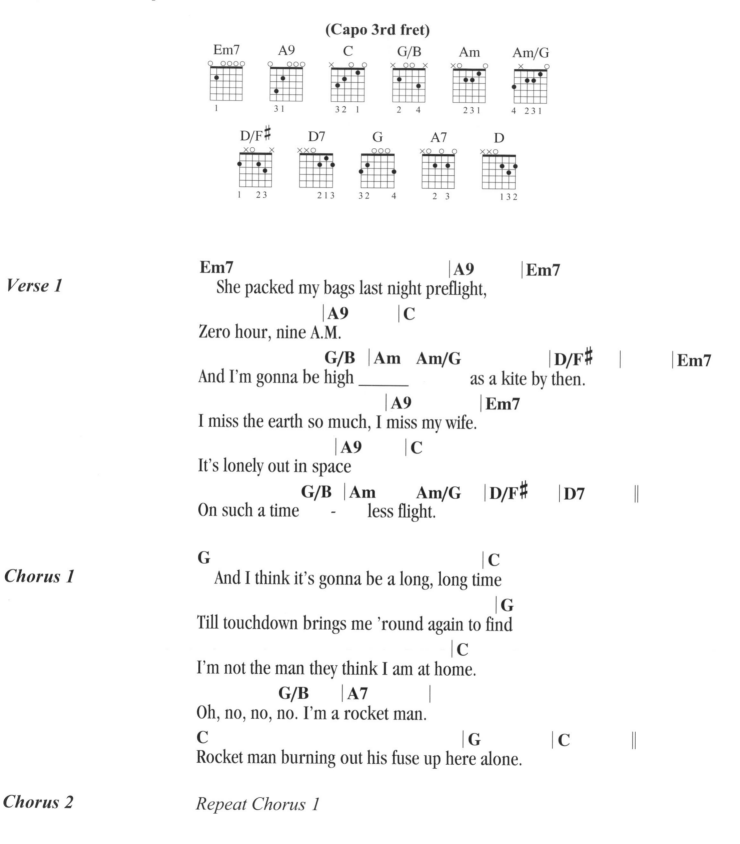

Verse 1

Em7 |A9 |Em7
  She packed my bags last night preflight,

     |A9 |C
Zero hour, nine A.M.

       G/B |Am Am/G |D/F♯ | |Em7
And I'm gonna be high _____   as a kite by then.

        |A9 |Em7
I miss the earth so much, I miss my wife.

      |A9 |C
It's lonely out in space

      G/B |Am Am/G |D/F♯ |D7 ||
On such a time - less flight.

Chorus 1

G |C
  And I think it's gonna be a long, long time

             |G
Till touchdown brings me 'round again to find

           |C
I'm not the man they think I am at home.

     G/B |A7 |
Oh, no, no, no. I'm a rocket man.

C |G |C ||
Rocket man burning out his fuse up here alone.

Chorus 2   *Repeat Chorus 1*

Verse 2

Em7 |A9 |Em7
   Mars ain't the kind of place to raise your kids,

               |A9 |C
In fact it's cold as hell.

                    G/B |Am Am/G |D/F♯ |D |Em7
And there's no one there to raise them   if you did.

                      |A9 |Em7
And all the science I don't understand,

                      |A9
It's just my job five days a week.

       |C   G/B |Am Am/G |D/F♯ |D   ‖
A rocket man, _____   a rocket man.

Chorus 3   *Repeat Chorus 1*

Chorus 4

G |C
   And I think it's gonna be a long, long time

                              |G
Till touchdown brings me 'round again to find

                         |C
I'm not the man they think I am at home.

          G/B |A7
Oh, no, no, no. I'm a rocket man.

C |G   ‖
Rocket man burning out his fuse up here alone.

Outro

‖: C |G   :‖
   And I think it's gonna be a long, long time.   *Repeat and fade*

Bennie and the Jets

Words and Music by
Elton John and Bernie Taupin

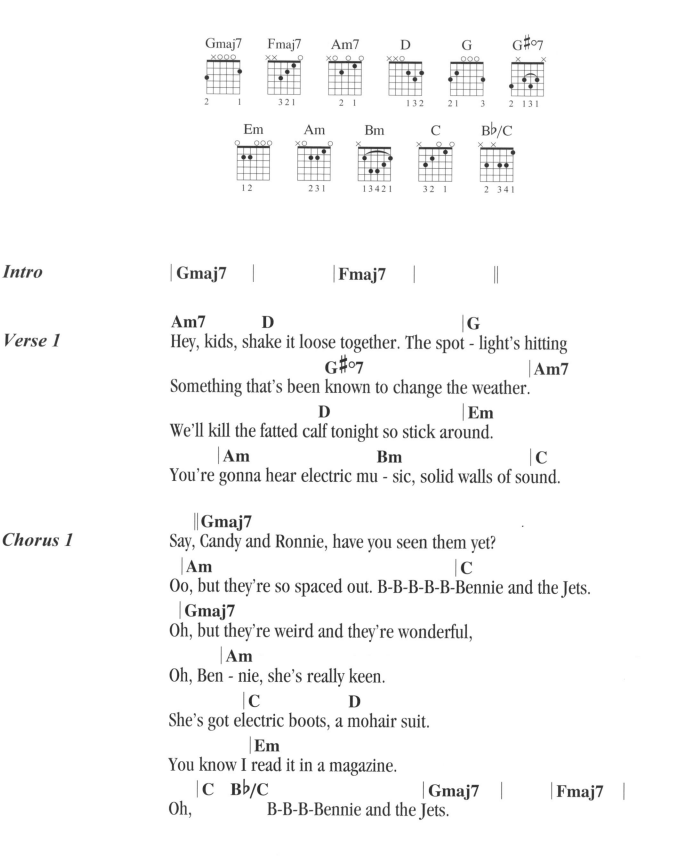

Intro
| Gmaj7 | | Fmaj7 | ||

Verse 1

Am7   D |G
Hey, kids, shake it loose together. The spot - light's hitting
                              G#°7 |Am7
Something that's been known to change the weather.
                         D |Em
We'll kill the fatted calf tonight so stick around.
     |Am   Bm |C
You're gonna hear electric mu - sic, solid walls of sound.

Chorus 1

‖Gmaj7
Say, Candy and Ronnie, have you seen them yet?
 |Am |C
Oo, but they're so spaced out. B-B-B-B-B-Bennie and the Jets.
  |Gmaj7
Oh, but they're weird and they're wonderful,
    |Am
Oh, Ben - nie, she's really keen.
         |C   D
She's got electric boots, a mohair suit.
           |Em
You know I read it in a magazine.
   |C   Bb/C |Gmaj7 | |Fmaj7 | ||
Oh,   B-B-B-Bennie and the Jets.

Verse 2

Am7   D |G
Hey, kids, plug into the faithless. May - be they're blinded
    G♯°7 |Am7
But Bennie makes them ageless.
                D |Em
We shall survive; let us take ourselves along.
        |Am   Bm
Where we fight our parents out in the streets

                      |C
To find who's right and who's wrong.

Chorus 2

        ‖Gmaj7
Oh, Candy and Ronnie, have you seen them yet?
 |Am |C
Oh, but they're so spaced out. B-B-B-B-B-Bennie and the Jets.
    |Gmaj7
Oh, but they're weird and they're wonderful.
        |Am
Oh, Ben - nie she's really keen.
        |C   D
She's got electric boots, a mohair suit.
            |Em
You know I read it in a magazine.
   |C   B♭/C |Gmaj7 | |Fmaj7 | ‖
Oh,   B-B-B-B-Bennie and the Jets.

Piano Solo   *Repeat Verse 1 (Instrumental)*

       ‖**Gmaj7**

Chorus 3   Oh, Candy and Ronnie, have you seen them yet?

     |**Am** |**C**

Oh, but they're so spaced out. B-B-B-B-B-B-Bennie and the Jets.

      |**Gmaj7**

Oh, but they're weird and they're wonderful,

         |**Am**

Oh, Ben - nie, she's really keen.

         |**C**   **D**

She's got electric boots, a mohair suit.

            |**Em**

You know I read it in a magazine.

    |**C** **B♭/C** |**Gmaj7** |

Oh,   B-B-B-Bennie and the Jets.

                      |**Fmaj7** | ‖

Bennie, Bennie and the Jets.

   ‖: **Gmaj7** | |**Fmaj7** | :‖

Outro   Bennie, Bennie, Bennie, Bennie and the Jets.   *Repeat and fade*

Don't Let the Sun Go Down on Me

Words and Music by
Elton John and Bernie Taupin

| C | C/B♭ | F | Dm | G | C/G | G7 |

| F/C | B♭ | Am7 | D7 | F/G | A♭6 |

Intro

‖ C   ‖ C/B♭   ‖ F   C   ‖ F   Dm ‖

Verse 1

G   C/G   ‖ G7
    I can't light

              ‖ F/C   C   ‖ F/C   C   ‖ F
No more of your dark   -   ness.

              ‖
All my pictures

                    ‖ G   C/G ‖ G   C/G ‖ G
Seem to fade to black and white.

           C/G   ‖ G7
I'm growing tired

            ‖ F/C   C   ‖   ‖ F
And time stands still be - fore me.

        B♭ ‖ F
Frozen here,

           ‖ G   C/G ‖ G   ‖
On the ladder of my life.

Verse 2

G   C/G |G7
  Too late

      |F/C C | |F
To save myself from fall - ing.

      B♭ |F
I took a chance

         |G C/G |G |G7
And changed your way of life.

     C/G |G
But you misread

       |F/C C | |F
My meaning when I met you.

      |
Closed the door

      |C/G |G F/G ‖
And left me blind - ed by the light.

Chorus 1

C |C/B♭ |Am7
  Don't let the sun go down on me.

Although I search myself,

   |D7 |C/G
It's always someone else I see.

        |F/G G
I'd just allow a fragment of your life

   |C |C/B♭
To wander free. _____

 |F
But losing ev'rything

   |Dm C F C/G F/G
Is like the sun go - ing down on…

Interlude |C |C/B♭ |F C |F Dm‖
         Me.

Verse 3

G   C/G |G7
    I can't find,

                         |F/C   C | |F
Oh, the right ro - mantic line.

                         |
But see me once

                       |G   C/G |G7 |
And see the way I feel.

                   C/G |G7
Don't discard me

                    |C | |F
Just because you think I mean you harm.

                      |
But these cuts I have,

                 |C/G |G   G7   ‖
Oh, they need love to help them heal.

Chorus 2   *Repeat Chorus 1*

Interlude |C |C/B♭ |F |A♭6 B♭ ‖
                        Me.

Chorus 3   *Repeat Chorus 1*

Outro |C |C/B♭ |F |A♭6 B♭ |C   ‖
                        Me.

Sorry Seems to Be the Hardest Word

Words and Music by
Elton John and Bernie Taupin

(Capo 3rd fret)

Em7   C#m7b5   Cmaj7   Em/B   Am7   F#m7b5   B7   Em

D   G   D/F#   C/E   B/D#   G/D   C

Intro

|Em7 C#m7b5|Cmaj7 Em/B |Am7 |F#m7b5 B7 ||

Verse 1

Em |Am7 |D
   What have I got to do to make you love me?
                                        |G   F#m7b5 B7 |Em
What have I got to do to make you care?
                                |Am7 |D
What do I do when lightning strikes me
                        |G   F#m7b5 B7 ||
And awake to find that you're not there?

Verse 2

Em |Am7 |D
   What do I do to make you want me?
                        |G   F#m7b5 B7 |Em
What have I got to do to be heard?
                        |Am7
What do I say when it's all over?
|D |G   D/F# ||
And sorry seems to be the hardest word.

Chorus 1

C/E   B/D♯ |G/D   C♯m7♭5 |C
It's sad, (It's so sad.) it's so sad,   it's a sad, sad situation
             B7 |Em   F♯m7♭5 B7 |C/E
And it's getting more and more absurd.
                  B/D♯ |G/D   C♯m7♭5 |C
It's sad, (It's so sad.) it's so sad,   why can't we talk it over?
                    |Am7   B7 ||
Oh, it seems to me that sorry seems to be the hardest word.

Interlude

|Em |Am7 |D |G   F♯m7♭5 B7 |
|Em |Am7 |D |G   D/F♯ ||

Chorus 2   *Repeat Chorus 1*

Outro

Em |Am7
  What do I do to make you love me?
|D |G   F♯m7♭5 B7 |Em
Oh, what have I got to do to be heard?
                |Am7 |
What do I do when lightning strikes me?
F♯m7♭5   B7 |
What have I got to do?
Em   Am7
What have I got to do?
   |F♯m7♭5   B7
When sorry seems to be the hardest…
|Em7 C♯m7♭5|Cmaj7 Em/B |F♯m7♭5 B7 |Em ||
 Word? _____

Goodbye Yellow Brick Road

Words and Music by
Elton John and Bernie Taupin

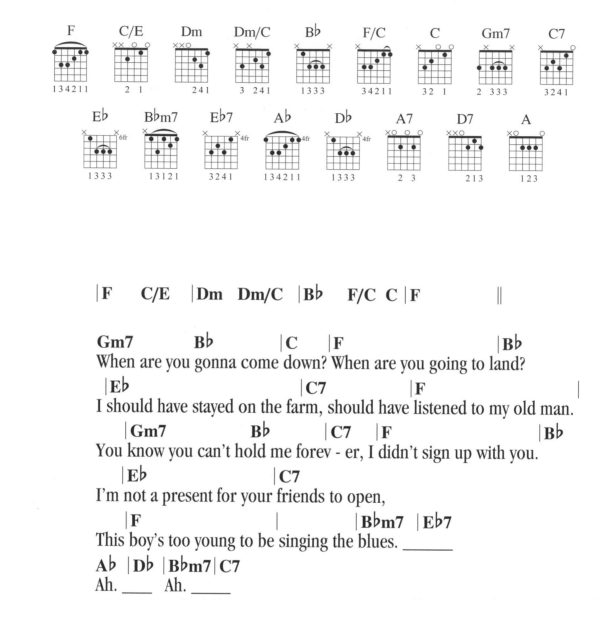

Intro |F C/E |Dm Dm/C |B♭ F/C C |F ||

Verse 1

Gm7   **B♭** |**C** |**F** |**B♭**
When are you gonna come down? When are you going to land?
  |**E♭** |**C7** |**F** |
I should have stayed on the farm, should have listened to my old man.
  |**Gm7**   **B♭** |**C7** |**F** |**B♭**
You know you can't hold me forev - er, I didn't sign up with you.
  |**E♭** |**C7**
I'm not a present for your friends to open,
  |**F** | |**B♭m7** |**E♭7**
This boy's too young to be singing the blues. _____
A♭ |**D♭** |**B♭m7**|**C7**
Ah. ____   Ah. _____

Chorus 1

‖**F** |**A7** |**B♭** |**F**
So goodbye yellow brick road where the dogs of society howl.

    |**D7** |**Gm7** |**C7** |**F**   **C/E** |
You can't plant me in your penthouse, I'm going back to my plough.

Dm |**A** |
Back to the howling old owl in the woods,

B♭ |**D♭** |
Hunting the homy back toad.

   E♭ |**F**   **C/E** |**Dm**   **Dm/C**
Oh, I've fin - 'ly decid - ed my future lies

  |**B♭**   **C7** |**B♭m7** |**E♭7**
Be - yond the yellow brick road. _____

A♭   **D♭** |**B♭m7** **C7** |**F** | ‖
Ah. ____   Ah. _____   Ah.

Verse 2

Gm7   **B♭** |**C** |**F** |**B♭**
What do you think you'll do then? I bet they shoot down your plane.

  |**E♭** |**C7** |**F** |
It'll take you a couple of vodka and tonics to set you on your feet again.

Gm7   **B♭** |**C7** |**F** |**B♭**
Maybe you'll get a replacement, there's plenty like me to be found.

E♭ |**C7** |
Mongrels who ain't got a penny

F | |**B♭m7** |**E♭7**
Sniffing for titbits like you on the ground.

A♭ |**D♭** |**B♭m7** **C7**
Ah. ____   Ah. _____

Chorus 2   *Repeat Chorus 1*

I'm Still Standing

Words and Music by
Elton John and Bernie Taupin

(Capo 1st fret)

Am   Dm/A   E/A   F/A   G/A   A   D   E

F#m   G6   Dm7   Fmaj7   G   E7   F

Intro

‖: Am   Dm/A | E/A | | F/A G/A :‖

Verse 1

     A | D
You could never know what it's like,
   | E | A
Your blood like winter freezes just like ice.
         | D | E
And there's a cold lonely light that shines from you;
     | F#m | D | A | ‖
You'll wind up like the wreck you hide behind that mask you use.

Verse 2

     A | D
   And did you think this fool could never win?
   | E | A
Well, look at me. I'm comin' back again.
   | D | E
I got a taste of love in a simple way,
     | F#m | D | A |
And if you need to know while I'm still standin', you just fade away.

Chorus 1

```
              ‖Am          |              |G6        |
Don't you know, I'm still standin' better than I ever did?
              |Dm7         |              |Fmaj7    |G
Looking like a true survivor, feeling like a little kid.
 |Am          |     |G6        |
I'm still standin' after all this time.
              |Dm7         |              |E7       |
Pickin' up the pieces of my life without you on my mind.
F   G         |Am  |Dm7       |E7       |
I'm still standin',     yeah, yeah, yeah.
F   G         |Am  |Dm7       |E7       |    F    G  ‖
I'm still standin',     yeah, yeah, yeah.
```

Verse 3

```
 A                      |D
  Once I never could hope to win,
        |E                         |A
You're starting down the road leaving me again.
        |D                  |      E
The threats you made were meant to cut me down.
        |F♯m            |D        |A              |
And if our love was just a circus you'd be a clown by now.
```

Chorus 2

```
 ‖Am          |              |G6        |
No, I'm still standin' better than I ever did.
              |Dm7         |              |Fmaj7    |G
Looking like a true survivor, feeling like a little kid.
 |Am                  |G6        |
I'm still standin' after all this time.
              |Dm7         |              |E7       |
Pickin' up the pieces of my life without you on my mind.
F   G         |Am  |Dm7       |E7       |
I'm still standin',     yeah, yeah, yeah.
F   G         |Am  |Dm7       |E7       |    F    G  ‖
I'm still standin,'     yeah, yeah, yeah.
```

Guitar Solo

```
|A        |D       |E       |A          |
|D        |E       |F♯m     |D          |
|A        |
```

Chorus 3

```
                           ‖Am      |              |G6      |
Don't you know that I'm still standin' better than I ever did?
                  |Dm7      |          |Fmaj7   |G
Looking like a true survivor, feeling like a little kid.
 |Am       |          |G6      |
I'm still standin' after all this time.
                  |Dm7       |              |E7        |
Pickin' up the pieces of my life without you on my mind.
F   G        |Am  |Dm7       |E7        |
I'm still standin',    yeah, yeah, yeah.
F   G        |Am  |Dm7       |E7        |
I'm still standin',    yeah, yeah, yeah.
F   G        |Am  |Dm7       |E7        |
I'm still standin',    yeah, yeah, yeah.
F   G        |Am  |Dm7       |E7        |
I'm still standin',    yeah, yeah, yeah.
F   G        |Am  |Dm7       |E7        |
I'm still standin',    yeah, yeah, yeah.
F   G        |Am       ‖
```

(I'm Gonna) Love Me Again

Words and Music by
Elton John and Bernie Taupin

Chord diagrams: C   A/C#   Dm   Fm   G7   G   Db   Ebm   Ab   Bbm   Db/Ab   Gb   F7   Gb/Ab

Intro

| | C | | | | | | | |
| | | | | | | | | |

Verse 1

‖ **C** |
Oh, the joke was never hard to tell.
|**A/C♯** |
Through my spare change in the wishing well.
|**Dm** |
The dream alone is all within your hand,
|**Fm** |**G7**
If that don't fill the boy and build the man.
|**C** |
A heart has many secrets, so I'm told.
|**A/C♯** |
Through the years, a theory can grow cold.
|**Dm** |
I'm out to beat the king, it's gotten clear.
|**Fm** |**G** ‖
The voice inside my head's the one I hear, saying:

Chorus 1

D♭ |
I'm gonna love me again,
    |**E♭m** |
Check in on my very best friend.
    |**A♭** |
Find the wind and fill my sails,
    |**D♭** |
Rise above the broken rails.
 |**B♭m** |**D♭/A♭** |
Unbound by any ties that break or bend,
  |**G♭** |
I'm free and don't you know.
 |**E♭m** |
No clown to claim he used to know me then.
 |**F7** |
I'm free, and don't you know.
  |**E♭m** **G♭** | **G♭/A♭** |**D♭** | | |
And oh, oh, oh, I'm gonna love me again.

Verse 2

    ‖**C** |
The Golden age was somehow bittersweet,
    |**A/C♯** |
But now the past lies sleeping in the deep.
 |**Dm** |
The peaceful days that followed hollow nights;
 |**Fm** |**G7**
A kiss or touch could feel like kryptonite.
    |**C** |
Praise the saints that hung up on my wall,
  |**A/C♯** |
For trust is left from lovers after all.
 |**Dm** |
A whispered word emerging from a tale,
 |**Fm** |**G**
My wakeup call to claim the curse dispelled.

Chorus 2

‖ **D♭** |
And I'm gonna love me again,
     | **E♭m** |
Check in on my very best friend.
      | **A♭** |
Find the wind and fill my sails,
      | **D♭** |
Rise above the broken rails.
     | **B♭m** | **D♭/A♭** |
Unbound by any ties that break or bend,
     | **G♭** |
I'm free and don't you know.
     | **E♭m** |
No clown to claim he used to know me then.
      | **F7** |
I'm free, and don't you know.
     | **E♭m**   **G♭** | **G♭/A♭** | **D♭** | ‖
And oh, oh, oh, I'm gonna love me again.

Instrumental

Repeat Verse 1

Chorus 3

D♭ |
I'm gonna love me again,
     | **E♭m** |
Check in on my very best friend.
      | **A♭** |
Find the wind and fill my sails,
      | **D♭** |
Rise above the broken rails.
     | **B♭m** | **D♭/A♭** |
Unbound by any ties that break or bend,
      | **G♭** |
I'm free and don't you know.
     | **E♭m** |
No clown to claim he used to know me then.
     | **F7** |
I'm free, and don't you know.
     | **E♭m** | |
And oh, oh, oh, oh, oh, oh, oh, oh, oh.
G♭ | **G♭/A♭**   ‖
I'm gonna love me again.

Outro

| **D♭** | | **G♭**
| **G♭/A♭** | **D♭** | | **B♭m**
I'm gonna love me again.
G♭ | **G♭/A♭** | **D♭** | | | ‖
I'm gonna love me again.

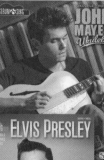

STRUM & SING

Lyrics, chord symbols, and guitar chord diagrams for your favorite songs.

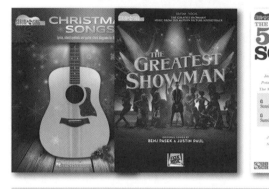

GUITAR

ACOUSTIC CLASSICS
00191891 .... $14.99

ADELE
00159855 .... $12.99

SARA BAREILLES
00102354 .... $12.99

THE BEATLES
00172234 .... $16.99

BLUES
00159335 .... $12.99

ZAC BROWN BAND
02501620 .... $14.99

COLBIE CAILLAT
02501725 .... $14.99

CAMPFIRE FOLK SONGS
02500686 .... $14.99

CHART HITS OF 2014-2015
00142554 .... $12.99

CHART HITS OF 2015-2016
00156248 .... $12.99

BEST OF KENNY CHESNEY
00142457 .... $14.99

CHRISTMAS SONGS
00171332 .... $14.99

KELLY CLARKSON
00146384 .... $14.99

COFFEEHOUSE SONGS FOR GUITAR
00285991 .... $14.99

LEONARD COHEN
00265489 .... $14.99

JOHN DENVER COLLECTION
02500632 .... $12.99

DISNEY
00233900 .... $16.99

EAGLES
00157994 .... $12.99

EASY ACOUSTIC SONGS
00125478 .... $14.99

THE 5 CHORD SONGBOOK
02501718 .... $12.99

FOLK SONGS
02501482 .... $10.99

FOLK/ROCK FAVORITES
02501669 .... $12.99

FOUR CHORD SONGS
00249581 .... $14.99

THE 4 CHORD SONGBOOK
02501533 .... $12.99

THE 4-CHORD COUNTRY SONGBOOK
00114936 .... $15.99

THE GREATEST SHOWMAN
00278383 .... $14.99

HAMILTON
00217116 .... $14.99

JACK JOHNSON
02500858 .... $17.99

ROBERT JOHNSON
00191890 .... $12.99

CAROLE KING
00115243 .... $10.99

BEST OF GORDON LIGHTFOOT
00139393 .... $14.99

DAVE MATTHEWS BAND
02501078 .... $10.95

JOHN MAYER
02501636 .... $10.99

INGRID MICHAELSON
02501634 .... $10.99

THE MOST REQUESTED SONGS
02501748 .... $12.99

JASON MRAZ
02501452 .... $14.99

PRAISE & WORSHIP
00152381 .... $12.99

ELVIS PRESLEY
00198890 .... $12.99

QUEEN
00218578 .... $12.99

ROCK AROUND THE CLOCK
00103625 .... $12.99

ROCK BALLADS
02500872 .... $9.95

ROCKETMAN
00300469 .... $17.99

ED SHEERAN
00152016 .... $14.99

THE 6 CHORD SONGBOOK
02502277 .... $12.99

CAT STEVENS
00116827 .... $14.99

TAYLOR SWIFT
00159856 .... $12.99

THE 3 CHORD SONGBOOK
00211634 .... $10.99

TODAY'S HITS
00119301 .... $12.99

TOP CHRISTIAN HITS
00156331 .... $12.99

TOP HITS OF 2016
00194288 .... $12.99

KEITH URBAN
00118558 .... $14.99

THE WHO
00103667 .... $12.99

YESTERDAY
00301629 .... $14.99

NEIL YOUNG – GREATEST HITS
00138270 .... $14.99

UKULELE

THE BEATLES
00233899 .... $16.99

COLBIE CAILLAT
02501731 .... $10.99

COFFEEHOUSE SONGS FOR UKULELE
00138238 .... $14.99

JOHN DENVER
02501694 .... $10.99

FOLK ROCK FAVORITES FOR UKULELE
00114600 .... $12.99

THE 4-CHORD UKULELE SONGBOOK
00114331 .... $14.99

JACK JOHNSON
02501702 .... $19.99

JOHN MAYER
02501706 .... $10.99

INGRID MICHAELSON
02501741 .... $12.99

THE MOST REQUESTED SONGS
02501453 .... $14.99

JASON MRAZ
02501753 .... $14.99

SING-ALONG SONGS
02501710 .... $15.99

HAL•LEONARD®

www.halleonard.com
Visit our website to see full song lists.

Prices, content, and availability subject to change without notice.

Guitar Chord Songbooks

Each 6" x 9" book includes complete lyrics, chord symbols, and guitar chord diagrams.

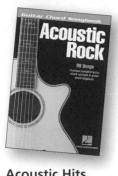
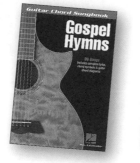
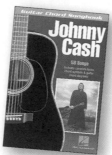
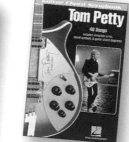

Acoustic Hits
00701787 . . . . $14.99

Acoustic Rock
00699540 . . . . $19.99

Alabama
00699914 . . . . $14.95

The Beach Boys
00699566 . . . . $17.99

The Beatles (A-I)
00699558 . . . . $17.99

The Beatles (J-Y)
00699562 . . . . $17.99

Bluegrass
00702585 . . . . $14.99

Johnny Cash
00699648 . . . . $17.99

Children's Songs
00699539 . . . . $16.99

Christmas Carols
00699536 . . . . $12.99

Christmas Songs – 2nd Edition
00119911 . . . . $14.99

Eric Clapton
00699567 . . . . $16.99

Classic Rock
00699598 . . . . $16.99

Coffeehouse Hits
00703318 . . . . $14.99

Country
00699534 . . . . $14.99

Country Favorites
00700609 . . . . $14.99

Country Hits
00140859 . . . . $14.99

Country Standards
00700608 . . . . $12.95

Cowboy Songs
00699636 . . . . $15.99

Creedence Clearwater Revival
00701786 . . . . $15.99

Jim Croce
00148087 . . . . $14.99

Crosby, Stills & Nash
00701609 . . . . $12.99

John Denver
02501697 . . . . $16.99

Neil Diamond
00700606 . . . . $17.99

Disney – 2nd Edition
00295786 . . . . $17.99

The Best of Bob Dylan
14037617 . . . . $17.99

Eagles
00122917 . . . . $16.99

Early Rock
00699916 . . . . $14.99

Folksongs
00699541 . . . . $14.99

Folk Pop Rock
00699651 . . . . $15.99

40 Easy Strumming Songs
00115972 . . . . $15.99

Four Chord Songs
00701611 . . . . $14.99

Glee
00702501 . . . . $14.99

Gospel Hymns
00700463 . . . . $14.99

Grand Ole Opry®
00699885 . . . . $16.95

Grateful Dead
00139461 . . . . $14.99

Green Day
00103074 . . . . $14.99

Guitar Chord Songbook White Pages
00702609 . . . . $29.99

Irish Songs
00701044 . . . . $14.99

Michael Jackson
00137847 . . . . $14.99

Billy Joel
00699632 . . . . $16.99

Elton John
00699732 . . . . $15.99

Ray LaMontagne
00130337 . . . . $12.99

Latin Songs
00700973 . . . . $14.99

Love Songs
00701043 . . . . $14.99

Bob Marley
00701704 . . . . $14.99

Bruno Mars
00125332 . . . . $12.99

Paul McCartney
00385035 . . . . $16.95

Steve Miller
00701146 . . . . $12.99

Modern Worship
00701801 . . . . $16.99

Motown
00699734 . . . . $17.99

Willie Nelson
00148273 . . . . $15.99

Nirvana
00699762 . . . . $16.99

Roy Orbison
00699752 . . . . $16.99

Peter, Paul & Mary
00103013 . . . . $14.99

Tom Petty
00699883 . . . . $15.99

Pink Floyd
00139116 . . . . $14.99

Pop/Rock
00699538 . . . . $16.99

Praise & Worship
00699634 . . . . $14.99

Elvis Presley
00699633 . . . . $15.99

Queen
00702395 . . . . $14.99

Red Hot Chili Peppers
00699710 . . . . $17.99

The Rolling Stones
00137716 . . . . $17.99

Bob Seger
00701147 . . . . $12.99

Carly Simon
00121011 . . . . $14.99

Sting
00699921 . . . . $14.99

Taylor Swift
00263755 . . . . $16.99

Three Chord Acoustic Songs
00123860 . . . . $14.99

Three Chord Songs
00699720 . . . . $14.99

Two-Chord Songs
00119236 . . . . $14.99

U2
00137744 . . . . $14.99

Hank Williams
00700607 . . . . $16.99

Stevie Wonder
00120862 . . . . $14.99

Neil Young–Decade
00700464 . . . . $15.99

Prices, contents, and availability subject to change without notice.

Visit Hal Leonard online at **www.halleonard.com**

EASY GUITAR
WITH NOTES & TAB

This series features simplified arrangements with notes, tab, chord charts, and strum and pick patterns.

MIXED FOLIOS

00702287	Acoustic	$16.99
00702002	Acoustic Rock Hits for Easy Guitar	$15.99
00702166	All-Time Best Guitar Collection	$19.99
00702232	Best Acoustic Songs for Easy Guitar	$14.99
00119835	Best Children's Songs	$16.99
00702233	Best Hard Rock Songs	$15.99
00703055	The Big Book of Nursery Rhymes & Children's Songs	$16.99
00322179	The Big Easy Book of Classic Rock Guitar	$24.95
00698978	Big Christmas Collection	$17.99
00702394	Bluegrass Songs for Easy Guitar	$12.99
00289632	Bohemian Rhapsody	$17.99
00703387	Celtic Classics	$14.99
00224808	Chart Hits of 2016-2017	$14.99
00267383	Chart Hits of 2017-2018	$14.99
00702149	Children's Christian Songbook	$9.99
00702028	Christmas Classics	$8.99
00101779	Christmas Guitar	$14.99
00702185	Christmas Hits	$10.99
00702141	Classic Rock	$8.95
00159642	Classical Melodies	$12.99
00253933	Disney/Pixar's Coco	$16.99
00702203	CMT's 100 Greatest Country Songs	$29.99

00702283	The Contemporary Christian Collection	$16.99
00196954	Contemporary Disney	$16.99
00702239	Country Classics for Easy Guitar	$22.99
00702257	Easy Acoustic Guitar Songs	$14.99
00702280	Easy Guitar Tab White Pages	$29.99
00702041	Favorite Hymns for Easy Guitar	$10.99
00222701	Folk Pop Songs	$14.99
00140841	4-Chord Hymns for Guitar	$9.99
00702281	4 Chord Rock	$10.99
00126894	Frozen	$14.99
00702286	Glee	$16.99
00699374	Gospel Favorites	$16.99
00702160	The Great American Country Songbook	$16.99
00702050	Great Classical Themes for Easy Guitar	$8.99
00702116	Greatest Hymns for Guitar	$10.99
00275088	The Greatest Showman	$17.99
00148030	Halloween Guitar Songs	$14.99
00702273	Irish Songs	$12.99
00192503	Jazz Classics for Easy Guitar	$14.99
00702275	Jazz Favorites for Easy Guitar	$15.99
00702274	Jazz Standards for Easy Guitar	$16.99
00702162	Jumbo Easy Guitar Songbook	$19.99
00232285	La La Land	$16.99
00702258	Legends of Rock	$14.99
00702189	MTV's 100 Greatest Pop Songs	$24.95

00702272	1950s Rock	$15.99
00702271	1960s Rock	$15.99
00702270	1970s Rock	$16.99
00702269	1980s Rock	$15.99
00702268	1990s Rock	$19.99
00109725	Once	$14.99
00702187	Selections from O Brother Where Art Thou?	$17.99
00702178	100 Songs for Kids	$14.99
00702515	Pirates of the Caribbean	$14.99
00702125	Praise and Worship for Guitar	$10.99
00287930	Songs from *A Star Is Born, The Greatest Showman, La La Land*, and More Movie Musicals	$16.99
00702285	Southern Rock Hits	$12.99
00156420	Star Wars Music	$14.99
00121535	30 Easy Celtic Guitar Solos	$15.99
00702220	Today's Country Hits	$12.99
00121900	Today's Women of Pop & Rock	$14.99
00244654	Top Hits of 2017	$14.99
00283786	Top Hits of 2018	$14.99
00702294	Top Worship Hits	$15.99
00702255	VH1's 100 Greatest Hard Rock Songs	$27.99
00702175	VH1's 100 Greatest Songs of Rock and Roll	$24.99
00702253	Wicked	$12.99

ARTIST COLLECTIONS

00702267	AC/DC for Easy Guitar	$15.99
00702598	Adele for Easy Guitar	$15.99
00156221	Adele – 25	$16.99
00702040	Best of the Allman Brothers	$16.99
00702865	J.S. Bach for Easy Guitar	$14.99
00702169	Best of The Beach Boys	$12.99
00702292	The Beatles — 1	$19.99
00125796	Best of Chuck Berry	$15.99
00702201	The Essential Black Sabbath	$12.95
02501615	Zac Brown Band — The Foundation	$16.99
02501621	Zac Brown Band — You Get What You Give	$16.99
00702043	Best of Johnny Cash	$16.99
00702090	Eric Clapton's Best	$12.99
00702086	Eric Clapton — from the Album Unplugged	$15.99
00702202	The Essential Eric Clapton	$14.99
00702250	blink-182 — Greatest Hits	$15.99
00702053	Best of Patsy Cline	$15.99
00222697	Very Best of Coldplay – 2nd Edition	$14.99
00702229	The Very Best of Creedence Clearwater Revival	$15.99
00702145	Best of Jim Croce	$15.99
00702278	Crosby, Stills & Nash	$12.99
14042809	Bob Dylan	$14.99
00702276	Fleetwood Mac — Easy Guitar Collection	$14.99
00139462	The Very Best of Grateful Dead	$15.99
00702136	Best of Merle Haggard	$14.99
00702227	Jimi Hendrix — Smash Hits	$16.99
00702288	Best of Hillsong United	$12.99
00702236	Best of Antonio Carlos Jobim	$14.99
00702245	Elton John — Greatest Hits 1970–2002	$17.99

00129855	Jack Johnson	$16.99
00702204	Robert Johnson	$10.99
00702234	Selections from Toby Keith — 35 Biggest Hits	$12.95
00702003	Kiss	$12.99
00702216	Lynyrd Skynyrd	$15.99
00702182	The Essential Bob Marley	$14.99
00146081	Maroon 5	$14.99
00121925	Bruno Mars – Unorthodox Jukebox	$12.99
00702248	Paul McCartney — All the Best	$14.99
00702129	Songs of Sarah McLachlan	$12.95
00125484	The Best of MercyMe	$12.99
02501316	Metallica — Death Magnetic	$19.99
00702209	Steve Miller Band — Young Hearts (Greatest Hits)	$12.95
00124167	Jason Mraz	$15.99
00702096	Best of Nirvana	$15.99
00702211	The Offspring — Greatest Hits	$12.95
00138026	One Direction	$14.99
00702030	Best of Roy Orbison	$15.99
00702144	Best of Ozzy Osbourne	$14.99
00702279	Tom Petty	$12.99
00102911	Pink Floyd	$16.99
00702139	Elvis Country Favorites	$16.99
00702293	The Very Best of Prince	$15.99
00699415	Best of Queen for Guitar	$15.99
00109279	Best of R.E.M.	$14.99
00702208	Red Hot Chili Peppers — Greatest Hits	$15.99
00198960	The Rolling Stones	$16.99
00174793	The Very Best of Santana	$14.99
00702196	Best of Bob Seger	$12.95
00146046	Ed Sheeran	$14.99
00702252	Frank Sinatra — Nothing But the Best	$12.99

00702010	Best of Rod Stewart	$16.99
00702049	Best of George Strait	$14.99
00702259	Taylor Swift for Easy Guitar	$15.99
00254499	Taylor Swift – Easy Guitar Anthology	$19.99
00702260	Taylor Swift — Fearless	$14.99
00139727	Taylor Swift — 1989	$17.99
00115960	Taylor Swift — Red	$16.99
00253667	Taylor Swift — Reputation	$17.99
00702290	Taylor Swift — Speak Now	$16.99
00232849	Chris Tomlin Collection – 2nd Edition	$14.99
00702226	Chris Tomlin — See the Morning	$12.95
00148643	Train	$14.99
00702427	U2 — 18 Singles	$16.99
00702108	Best of Stevie Ray Vaughan	$16.99
00279005	The Who	$14.99
00702123	Best of Hank Williams	$14.99
00194548	Best of John Williams	$14.99
00702111	Stevie Wonder — Guitar Collection	$9.95
00702228	Neil Young — Greatest Hits	$15.99
00119133	Neil Young — Harvest	$14.99

Prices, contents and availability subject to change without notice.

HAL•LEONARD®

Visit Hal Leonard online at **halleonard.com**